EXPLORING PATCHWORK

EXPLORING PATCHWORK

Doris E. Marston

author of
Patchwork Today: A Practical Introduction

LONDON: G. BELL & SONS LTD

A Bell Handbook

ISBN O 7135 1697 6

PRINTED IN GREAT BRITAIN AT
the St. Ann's Press, Park Road,
Altrincham, Cheshire WA14 5QQ

Contents

Acknowledgments

The author wishes to express her thanks to all those W.I. friends who so kindly lent patchwork to provide the illustrations for this book; to her son, who generously gave much time to photographing most of them; to her husband, who checked the scripts; and to Mrs Josie Buckland, who once again typed them. She is indebted also to Messrs Heinemann, London, and Doubleday & Co., Inc., New York, publishers, for permission to use the quotation from Wm E. Barrett's book, *A Woman in the House*.

1. Exploring patchwork

However much one is attracted to a craft, it is not possible to realise its full potentialities until the initial techniques have been learned. It is from knowledge, practice with experiment, that the love and full enjoyment of a craft grow.

Patchwork appears to have unlimited potentialities and surely there is no other craft that can be adapted so well to so many needs or that looks so right in so many places. Each generation, as time has passed, has used patchwork in its own way, suiting it to the fashion of the times and making it in the materials then available.

Over the ages, a variety of geometrical shapes have been selected for use as patchwork templates. Along with those we regard as basic shapes—hexagon, diamond and clamshell—are many more, less familiar, yet producing a recognisable effect in patchwork design.

Most of us who have made patchwork our favourite craft have a preference for certain templates and use them for most of our work. This tends to restrict our designing. We can all benefit from the change which experimenting with fresh templates brings.

A combination of templates is often the solution to our struggle to fit a design into an area of awkward shapes. Determination plus imagination are often needed to achieve our ends, but one generally feels afterwards that something worthwhile has been learned.

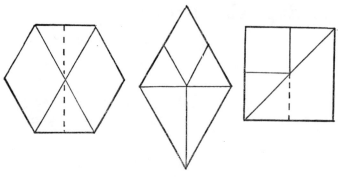

Diagram 1

A large hexagon, a square and a diamond are all divisible into smaller shapes, which can be combined with them in the same piece of work (Diagram 1).

The small cushion (Plate 1a) shows how effective the result can be. The shapes of large and small diamonds and triangles have been cut from a variety of textures and colours. The large patches shade from deepest purple to warm bright red and are a perfect setting for the small silk diamonds and triangles that, in clear pinks, reds and lilac shades, form the focal point of the design. There is tremendous scope for exploration with colour and texture in patchwork today, with all the variety of fabrics now at our disposal.

Even with some experience, designing for some of us remains the hard part of patchwork. Here again it may be good to break away from our preferences in patterned materials and, if we have designed mainly in the pretty flowery prints and chintzes, to try out something involving stripes, spots or other geometric patterns. This can be great fun and delightfully intriguing. If you can develop a 'jigsaw' imagination, combinations of portions of spots, or stripes and squares lying at unusual angles on adjoining patches, can be built up into unexpectedly exciting arrangements. It is better not to mentally pigeon-hole the different types of designs on our fabrics—so often they will work out well together if skilfully used and a more striking piece of work will result.

Simplicity of outline is usually the basis of a good design, and it is as well to have a clear mental picture of it, or even to draw it out and colour it, before commencing. This helps to achieve good proportion and balance, even though fresh ideas are almost certain to develop as one progresses. If one works to a chart, it is important to select one's materials beforehand, so that their effect on each other can be borne in mind while planning.

Like all crafts, patchwork is a means of self-expression and it is important to be original. It is tremendously satisfying to make something which is our own from start to finish—to know that we have created a thing which is unique and not simply a copy of someone else's work.

2. The clamshell—various techniques

There is no doubt that, of all the patchwork shapes, the clamshell is the most difficult. Its technique demands concentration and a great deal of patience in the early stages, when the patches are assembled. But no other template offers so many variations in arrangement, and it also has the virtue of covering the ground quickly.

The most familiar technique has been described in detail in *Patchwork Today,* but there are two others—the first similar in effect and usage, the second quite different, both in the construction of patches and in the joining-up process.

Technique No. 1: the usual method of construction (Diagram 2a)

The card, which is an exact replica of the solid template, is pinned into the right side of the patch of material. The semicircular edge is turned down, finely pleated and tacked down, following the curve of the card and matching it exactly. As each patch is made, the card is unpinned and used in the same way for succeeding patches.

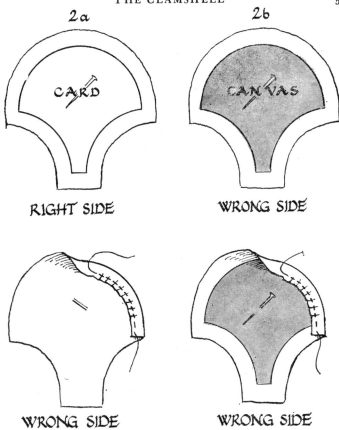

2a

2b

CARD

CANVAS

RIGHT SIDE

WRONG SIDE

WRONG SIDE

WRONG SIDE

Diagrams 2a and 2b

Technique No. 2 (Diagram 2b)

(a) To make the patches, replicas of the solid templates are cut out very exactly from tailor's canvas or vilene; one is needed for each patch. Patches are cut from the window template, as usual.

(b) Each lining is pinned into the wrong side of a patch and, as in the first method, the curved edge is pleated and stitched down by tacking (basting) into the lining material

Assembling patches, techniques 1 & 2

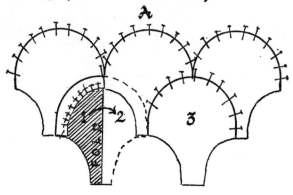

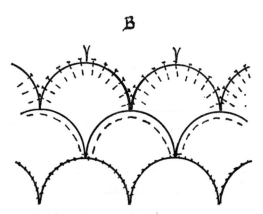

Diagrams 3a and 3b

—BUT the needle does not stitch through to the right side.

(c) Patches are then laid out in rows, in the usual way, following the plan of design, the raw edges of the stems being covered by the scallops of the succeeding rows in unbroken line (Diagrams 3a and 3b).

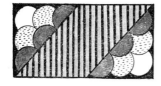

Diagram 4

Naturally, the permanently-lined patches produce a firm piece of work which keeps its shape well. The clearly-tailored clamshells are particularly suitable for anything like tea or coffee cosies or articles of any type where firmness enhances shapeliness.

Because of the emphasis that the linings give to the semi-circular patches, it is worthwhile to choose patterned materials whose units can fit into this outline. Designs which are based on rounded, flowing shapes turn out well.

Remember that the clamshells should, wherever possible, be marked out with the grain of the material running down the centre. Loosely-woven fabrics are not suitable and cottons are the best. It is possible with a three-inch template to use some of the heavier cottons and linens.

Designing using techniques 1 and 2

Most of us have learned to put our clamshell patches in horizontal rows, building our designs on lines which are mainly vertical or oblique—not realising that, by using a little imagination, we can group our patches to produce far more interesting results. It is quite unnecessary for the scalloped line to be horizontal—it, too, can lie in as many directions as the pattern (Diagram 4).

In all the arrangements illustrated, it is obvious that it is the plan of colour and pattern which creates an effective design. Good contrasts, or colours which pleasantly complement each other, together with pattern units which fit snugly into the arc-shaped top of the patch, are the most rewarding.

Fussy, indeterminate patterned materials do not mean much, because they do not emphasise the scalloped outline, which is the chief characteristic of this way of doing patchwork.

The articles made of clamshells are usually of a modest size, but if we intend to make something large—a quilt or a garment for an adult, for instance—then the patches should be joined into groups or blocks of convenient size before they are finally joined to fill the required area. A pair of large bed-curtains in the Victoria and Albert Museum,

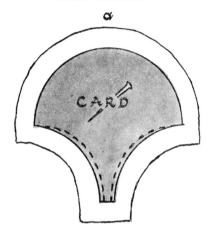

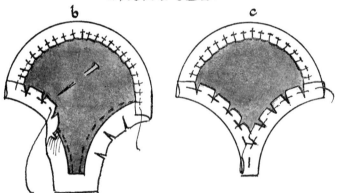

Diagram 5

made from clamshell patches in the late Stuart period, illustrate this method. Each group of patches was bound with ribbon before being sewn to its neighbour. Since the cottons used to make them are patterned in tiny floral designs, the bindings contribute greatly to the character of the patchwork.

B

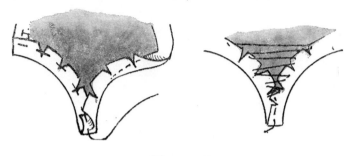

Diagram 6

Technique No. 3

By this method, the window and solid templates are used as for any other shape. The firmer greetings cards provide excellent papers over which to make patches, which must be turned down all round the shape, fitting it with great accuracy. A slender-stemmed clamshell must be used for this technique. Alternatively, cards cut from a broad-stemmed shape *must* be trimmed as shown by dotted lines (Diagram 5).

It is important, when drawing round the window, to mark out the bottom edge of the stem. Try to place the template on the grain of the material. This is easy with a plain fabric but not always possible with patterned.

Follow the diagrams for constructing a patch. Begin folding over and pleating the curved edge and continue round the stems, clipping the raw edges when necessary so that the folds fit the cards closely. Make the tiny turning of the stem base as neat as possible. Unwrinkled, accurately made patches facilitate joining. One must discover the method of tacking through the turnings-down which suits one best and which produces the best shapes. The diagrams show the two alternatives (Diagram 6).

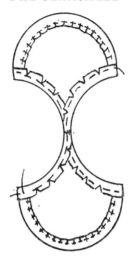

Diagram 7

Joining-up

This is done on the wrong side, as in other shapes, but because every edge of the clamshell is part of a circle (except for the base of the stem), it is obvious that seams must be made by ladder-stitch or slip-stitch, for oversewing is impossible, except for the tiny edges which lie across the stem.

It is here that joining-up begins (Diagram 7).

The next patch (or pair of patches) is fitted into the semi-circular space created by the seam. Fitting must be done with precision (Diagram 8) and the edges to be joined held a little apart so that the needle is slipped across from one to the other, to make many small neat stitches. When several have been made, the thread is tightened so that the folds are drawn absolutely together and the stitches lie hidden (Diagram 9).

The patchwork is continued by filling the semicircular spaces with more patches, which, the diagram shows, lie in

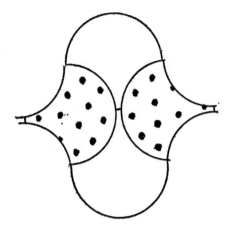

Diagram 8

Diagram 9

Diagram 10

four different positions. When the required amount has been done, the papers are removed and suitable finishings applied.

Odd as it may seem, this technique with the clamshell is actually preferred by some of us, who do not find it nearly so tricky as it appears. One must admit that the lovely meandering effect of this arrangement of the patches is very fascinating and there is great satisfaction in mastering the technique. The secret of success lies in choice of materials— they must be firm in weave and smoothly textured (Diagram 10).

3. Less popular shapes

Goose Track, Grandmother's Choice, Old Maid's Puzzle, Robbing Peter to Pay Paul are four names taken at random from the hundreds given to American block quilt patterns. These share a common factor, in that their designs are all based on squares and triangles, alone or in combination.

Designs such as these form a very large group from among those made using geometrical shapes. Many are old enough to have originated in England or Holland, from where they travelled across the sea to America with the early settlers.

The square, with the assorted shapes and sizes of triangles that can be made from it by folding or dividing, provides a tremendous field for inventiveness; the women of the past seem to have explored it thoroughly, producing an inheritance of intriguing and frequently beautiful patchwork. The effectiveness of these designs is due not only to their technical excellence but also to the clear and simple colour schemes in which they are created.

White was a favourite background for the bold reds, blues, oranges, and even blacks, which were among the popular traditional colours used for the designs. The material was frequently patterned, but never so boldly that the character of the design became lost. One's imagination is stimulated whenever one sees examples of this patchwork, for it is impossible not to visualise the enjoyable arranging

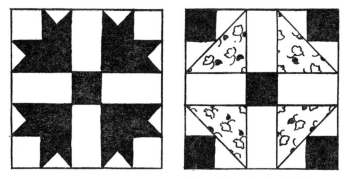

Diagram 11: (left) *Goose Tracks*, (right) *Grandmother's Choice.*

Diagram 12: (left) *Old Maid's Puzzle*, (right) *Robbing Peter to Pay Paul.*

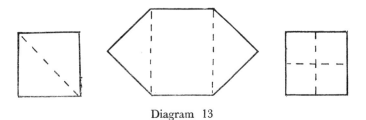

Diagram 13

and re-arranging that must have taken place before the
shapes fitted together satisfactorily.

The names, too, are a delight. *Grandmother's Choice* is
easy—obviously she liked that arrangement best. But who
gave the somewhat acid title to *Old Maid's Puzzle,* and
why? And whose quick wit thought up the name of
Robbing Peter to Pay Paul? (Diagrams 11 and 12).

The shapes

The square

The square patch is a fairly easy shape to make and in large
sizes can be made very well without a paper lining. The
simple chequer-board effect of white squares alternating
with black or any other colour is always arresting, though
in a large, all-over design it can be overwhelming and
monotonous. In the Victorian quilts, however, a check
border is frequently used attractively.

A red and white check bedspread made in Northamptonshire, England, around the middle of the 19th century had
the clear outline of a graceful flower spray, embroidered in
stem-stitch on each square, with an outline in back-stitch
$\frac{1}{4}$ of an inch within each seam join. On the red squares,
this was stitched in white thread, on white squares in red,
and it was pretty enough to make the bedspread something
out of the ordinary.

The lid of the large box in plate 2 is covered by patchwork made in rayon materials of various textures, in a
colour scheme of purples, grey and lime green. It is an
example of combined angular shapes used with good effect
in a strong colour scheme. Both the small squares and the
triangular patches are sub-divisions of the larger square
and the church windows are, in size, a combination of the
square and two triangles (Diagram 13).

The right angle of the triangular patch presents no difficulty when the patches are made, but the folding of turnings

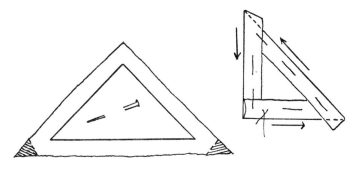

Diagram 14

at the sharp points is something of a problem. For constructing the patch, use a thin card for linings, and a firm, non-fraying material. With such fine points it is not possible to make a double fold, as with a diamond, but one can reduce the surplus of material by trimming some away (Diagram 14). Before using any of the man-made materials, it is wise to test their non-fraying qualities by cutting out a patch and making it up in this shape.

The Long Diamond

This is narrower than the diamond, which can be made by dividing a hexagon into three equal parts, and, like the previous shape, has two extremely fine points. It is the basis for the *Star of Bethlehem* quilt design which appears among both the English and American quilt patterns. Though it is not popular as a modern quilt design, one occasionally still comes across it. It demonstrates the same practical principle of extending the central eight-point star by adding row after row of patches, until the huge star fills most of the required area. This same design is sometimes seen in American books under the name of the *Lone Star* and there are also other variations of the theme which are still called the *Star of Bethlehem*.

It was, and is, a convenient way of using up oddments of

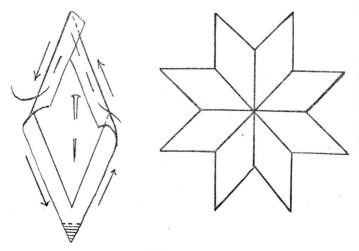

Diagram 15

material in an uncomplicated way for those who love
making the long diamond patch. The spaces between the
points of the huge star were usually filled in with light-
coloured plain patches, which enhanced the attractiveness
of the shape. This fitted well into a large square quilt,
suitable for a double bed.

The fact that, for most patchworkers, the long diamond
is one of the least favoured of the templates is because, like
the triangle, it needs the right type of material and great
precision to make a good patch and the points present a
similar difficulty, in that there is a good deal of surplus
material showing when folding has been completed. Unless
these points are accurately constructed, an eight-point star
will never lie as flat as it should when the patches have been
joined. Only the firm prints, sateens and chintzes make up
well in this shape. A neat, sharply-pointed patch, made
and joined up with great precision, will produce a first-rate
star, something to be proud of (Diagram 15).

Apart from *Star of Bethlehem* quilts, it is most unusual

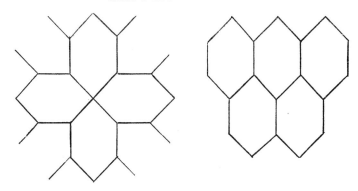

Diagram 16

to see the long diamond used by itself. It is when one is exploring a combination of shapes—those of squares, octagons and church windows—that its usefulness becomes apparent. So often, one finds that it is this one which will fit into an unexpected gap or complete the line of design in a satisfactory or exciting way.

The Church Window

This is a hexagon which has been slightly compressed so that, although the sides remain of equal length, the angles are altered. It is as uncomplicated as the hexagon patch to make and it is a particularly favourite shape for exploration, for even alone it can be arranged to produce two different effects. A square with sides of identical length will combine with it, and it follows that all other shapes derived from it can be combined (Diagram 16). One of these is—

The Octagon

This is a template which has to be used with a square and in this combination is to be seen more frequently as a tile pattern than in patchwork. It is, however, worth trying out. Although in large sizes it is not so easy to make well, it does

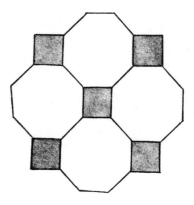

Diagram 17

possess the advantage of covering an area quickly (Diagram 17). The octagon-square combination can be very effective when used for silks and velvets, to produce the impression of a rich, embossed design in these two textures. Both church window and octagon lend themselves to ecclesiastical patchwork and, indeed, to any piece of work where a more formal design is appropriate. They have a particular usefulness in decorative borders, as well as part of an all-over pattern (Diagram 18). There is a great advantage in using patchwork in this way, in both the pieced and

Diagram 18

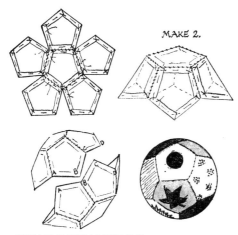

MAKE 2.

REMOVE PAPERS AS JOINING IS
DONE. LEAVE OPENING, TURN
TO RIGHT SIDE & COMPLETE.

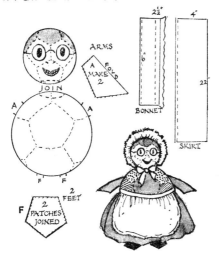

Diagram 19. *Granny Smith* doll:
Template for head ¾ of an inch ⎫ pentagon
Template for body and limbs 1¾ inches ⎰

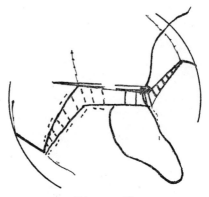

Diagram 20

Diagram 21

applied form, for it has an immediate effect and looks well in so many places. It would take very much more time and effort for embroidery to achieve the same result.

Pentagons

The patches of an equal-sided pentagon can never lie flat when they are joined together. Twelve of them make the familiar shape of a ball, so this template is generally used

Diagram 22

Diagram 23

for toy-making. A small patchwork ball, placed on top of a large one and joined securely to it, can be turned into a variety of chubby attractive character dolls (Diagram 19). Appropriate colours and materials should be selected for patches that are to simulate flesh, hair or costume. The features can either be embroidered or painted and limbs and 'feet' can be added if necessary. Any further dressing-up should be in character and kept as simple as possible.

Stuffing for both balls and dolls should be light and washable. Latex or plastic foam chippings are both good, especially for a ball which is to be played with. Packed in really tightly, it will be safe and bounceable. Terylene down or raw, washed sheep's wool are good fillings for dolls and both will restore to shape after washing. It is important to stuff the dolls as full as possible, using small amounts and packing in from the back to the front of the interior, using perhaps fingers at first, but later the blunt end of a pencil, the handle of a wooden spoon or a thick knitting needle. Only then make the final seam of ladder stitches (Diagram 20).

Another pentagonal shape is basically a broad diamond from which one sharp point has been trimmed. It can be used with a hexagon at the centre to make another type of six-point star (Diagram 21) or, with points to centre, can create a motif which will combine with hexagons (Diagram 22). Each of these arrangements are pretty enough in themselves to make them useful in many ways for producing needlecases, vanity cases, pincushions, and so on (Diagram 23).

In large templates, they can be used as decoration on stool-tops and cushions.

1a. Silk and velvet cushion in rich brown, purple and bright pink. *Miss Anne Dyer, Shropshire.*

1b. Cushion in orange and olive green cottons. *Mrs K. Thomson, Leics. and Rutland.*

2. Box top in rayons, purples, grey and lime. *Author*.

3. Linen cushion cover in crimson, green and blue, on natural ground. *Mrs Evans, Somerset.*

4. Navy slip for child, decorated with clamshell border. *Mrs Evans, Somerset.*

5a. Clamshell tea-cosy, turquoise, gold and white. *Mrs Thomson.*

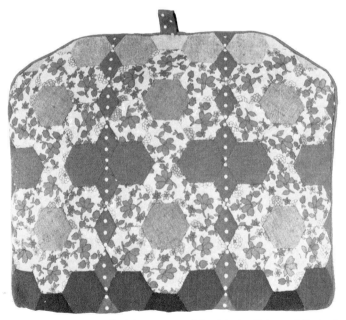

5b. Orange, green and white tea-cosy. *Mrs Atherley, Leics. and Rutland.*

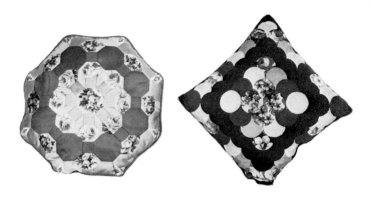

6. Patterned cushions, using octagon, church windows and squares. Clamshell and circle. *Mrs P. Edwards, Dorset.*

7. 'Jane's cushion'—navy, figures in suitable colours. *Mrs M. Ashmore, Northamptonshire.*

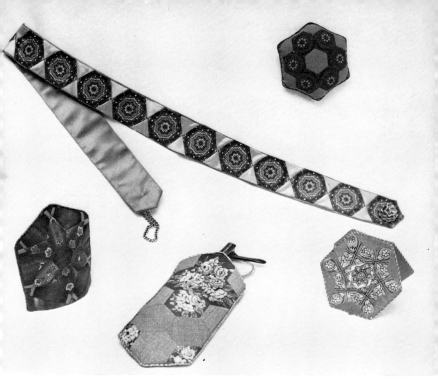

8. A belt, and other small things. *The author.*

9. Two cushions, church window, octagon and squares. Clamshell and circle. *Mrs Whittle, Oxfordshire, and Mrs Arnold, West Kent.*

10. Handbag in fur patchwork, lined with suede. *Mrs Organ, Leics. and Rutland.*

4. Patchwork stars—making and using them

'I saw a little star and it wunk at me,' says the small girl in Walter de la Mare's play, *Crossings*. It is from just a magical moment that the attraction of the star shape begins for most of us, remaining ever after a symbol of something bright and alluring. In patchwork, the star is represented in a hundred ways and has as many names, some associated with historic or social events or having geographical or legendary connections. Many of the traditional star-block patterns are extremely complicated, but it is basic star shapes that concern us now.

Six-point star
The six-point is the best known and most popular star and there are several variations. One has already been described in the previous chapter, but the six-point made from diamond patches is the one usually seen and the easiest to make. In the old quilts, its shape was used as a unit of an appliquéd border, in which the stars were hemmed down to the unbleached calico foundation. Another, far more complicated modern version, is made from a set or group of templates (see Catalogue at back of book, Set 11 and 12). In the two versions illustrated, the star centre is emphasised by the four-sided shapes on either side of the points (Diagram 24). These four-sided shapes must be very accurately

c

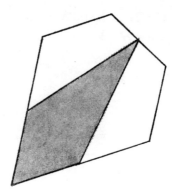

Diagram 24

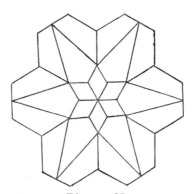

Diagram 25

made if they are to fit well. This combination makes a most attractive motif which looks well as a single decoration or as part of a larger design (Diagram 25 and Plate 12).

Hexagons and triangles compose another six-point star—less graceful and perhaps conveying the impression of a sun rather than a star (Diagram 26). The quilt books show many variations and one of them bears the title *Star of Bethlehem,* as a block pattern.

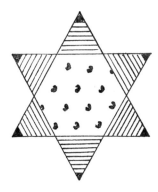

Diagram 26

Diagram 27

Four-point star
Four 'church-window' patches, joined points to centre,
form a cross. When the spaces between are filled by four
more patches (as in Diagram 27), a heavier star-like motif
is created. Although it lacks the 'twinkle' of the diamond
stars, this motif can be quite useful as the jumping-off
point for a large design or as a decoration for the top of a
square box.

Diagram 28

Diagram 29

Eight-point star

An English quilt made in Durham in 1890 has an all-over
design made up of eight-point stars, using a square as
centre and broad triangles as points (Diagram 28). In
America, this is a traditional pattern, sometimes called *Lone
Star* or *Saw Tooth*. Once again, the variations are many.

Diagram 30

Five-point star
A five-point star (Diagram 29) is perhaps the shape we see
most frequently on our Christmas cards or cut out in bright
foil for use with our decorations. This, too, can be made in
patchwork. In America, it bears the name *Union Star* and
its block pattern marks an historical event.

Having discovered the many ways of making patchwork
stars, let us consider how they may be used, not in quilt
patterns only, but by themselves, giving them full decorative
value.

It is far easier to make a star in patches for purposes of
appliqué than to cut out the whole thing from a single
piece of material. Even in plain colours, its prettiness will
be apparent, but the examples (Diagram 30) show how

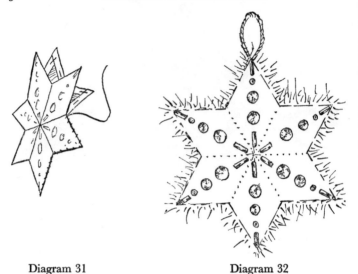

Diagram 31   Diagram 32

much can be done to make them even more fascinating, using different types of patterned fabrics. Exploration really pays in this particular field, for as a decorative motif the star has few rivals and many uses.

Stars for Christmas decorations

These can be as pretty and sparkling as you care to make them and will last for years if dusted and stored in a box between festivals.

You will need:

1. Any gaily-coloured scraps of material, though silks and lurex fabrics are best of all

2. Thin but firm card over which to make patches and leave in

3. Metal or silk cord to make loop by which to hang the star when finished

Diagram 33

4. Beads, sequins or baubles to add sparkle

Make two stars, using six diamond patches for each and
cutting patches from the same template. Stitch on any beads
or sequins. Place stars together with wrong sides inside and
oversew or finely slip-stitch together, making them fit exactly
(Diagram 31).

Decorate edges with couching—tinsel can be stitched
round by this method, if you wish. Make a loop, and the
star is ready to hang (Diagram 32).

A starry hanging

This is a gauzy banner which can be suspended freely, like
a mobile, or displayed on a wall (Diagram 33).

Diagram 34

Its shape and size depend on the individual, but its length and width should be in proportion: the length roughly twice the width is a good guide.

The size of the template for each star needs to be carefully chosen with regard to its proportion. A variety of sizes can produce attractive 'constellations' if their planning has been well thought out. If you have no ideas of your own, a version of a real one will do very well!

Step-by-step instructions:

(*a*) For the foundation, choose a piece of gauzy transparent material—terylene curtain-net or tulle. Cut it to required size, making allowances for hems $\frac{3}{4}$ of an inch at sides, $1\frac{1}{4}$ inches at top and 1 inch at bottom. Leave any selvedges unturned but stitch hems down decoratively and neatly, and press.

(*b*) Make single six-point stars, as many as you need. Lay foundation down in a flat surface and plan the arrangement, marking with chalk or pencil the place of each star. It helps to put a dab of non-liquid glue on the wrong side of the star to hold it in place before tacking into position prior to hemming. Alternatively, the whole star may be stuck down, so long as this is done securely.

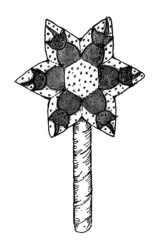

Diagram 35

(c) For a free hanging, make matching star to sew or stick to the reverse side. This is not necessary if it is to be displayed against a wall.

(d) Slide a cane or smooth rod of the right size through the top hem and tie tinsel cord or ribbon to either end.

Another pretty way of making a star decoration is to use a lampshade ring bound with tinsel or ribbon, from which stars can be suspended at varying heights (Diagram 34).

Decorations in many other shapes may be made in patchwork just as easily, for display about the house or on the Christmas tree.

Baby's rattle

This time made from six-point stars, using a hexagon and pentagon, as illustrated (Diagram 35).

You will need :

1. Strong, gay print

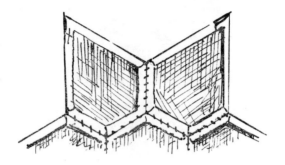

Diagram 36

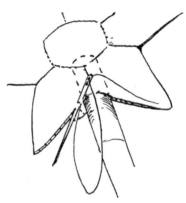

Diagram 37

2. Tailor's canvas, hat buckram or card
3. Small scraps of plastic foam sheeting, terylene wadding (batting) or any other washable filling
4. A strip of wood $\frac{3}{4}$ of an inch wide and 9–10 inches long, or a piece of dowelling $\frac{1}{2}$ an inch in diameter (a lolly stick can be used for the strip).
5. A small plastic box (or tin) to hold beads, peas, seeds for rattle or, failing this, two or three small bells tied in a plastic bag.
Make the two stars.

If using foam, cut twelve shapes, using the pentagon templates, and stick them down tightly on the wrong side of each point. Trim down edges of the foam shapes (Diagram 36).

Join the stars together by ladder-stitch or oversewing, leaving two edges of a pair of points open for further stuffing and the box and stick.

Push a little more filling into all points, using a blunt knitting pin, insert box and more filling, if necessary, then insert stick (already covered with ribbon or strips of material or patchwork) and stitch in very securely (Diagram 37). Complete joining-up of star.

This is a safe, washable toy for a small baby.

5. Making and covering a box

To make a box and cover it, or to cover one already made, is a challenge few needlewomen can resist. There is enormous satisfaction in producing one which is both attractive and has a truly professional appearance.

The secret lies in having a clear mental picture of what one is aiming at and planning thoroughly before one begins.

The preliminary measuring and fitting must be precise and the covering materials should be chosen for wearability as well as appearance. Materials which are coarse and fray easily, or others which are too delicate, will be useless.

The lid may be flat and either hinged or made separate to fit over the top. If hinged, a fastening may be needed; if separate, a knob or ring would be practical for lifting.

Patchwork, both pieced and applied, has an immediate decorative effect and lends itself admirably to be used as a covering. Templates must be chosen so that their size and shape will produce a covering to fit the area of the box.

The lining for the inside is as important as the outer cover and should be as carefully chosen. A thin, firm material, such as percale, is excellent. If a spongeable lining is preferred, there are several plastic materials on the market of the right weight. Padding can be made from flannelette, terylene wadding (batting) or thin, plastic foam sheeting laid beneath the lining.

You will need:

1. A strong, sharp modelling knife or penknife
2. Pencil and ruler
3. Glue or gum—any clear, non-liquid, non-staining one will do (Uhu, Gripfix, etc.)
4. Cartridge paper or thin card for making patterns or drawing plan
5. Templates for decoration or patchwork
6. Materials: for cover
              for lining
              any fasteners needed
7. Card—strawboard or something else equally rigid but not too thick.

Choose fasteners according to the purpose for which the box will be used: press studs (as used in leather work), button and loop and velcro are all good in the right places.

Covering a square box with a hinged lid

Directions are given for a box 5 inches square, 2 inches deep.
Cut card as follows:

4 pieces for sides, 5 inches by 2 inches ⎞ all in
1 piece for base, 5 inches by 5 inches ⎬ strong
1 piece for lid, 5 1/10 inches square ⎠ card
1 piece thin card, 5 inches square, for lid lining

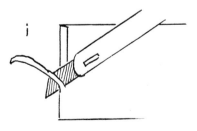
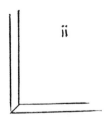

Diagram 38

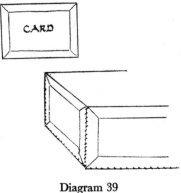

Diagram 39

Slightly shave down the narrow inside edges of each piece and mark that side with pencil, as in Diagram 38(i)—this is to make a good right angle when fitted together: Diagram 38(ii).

Using a side-piece, the base and the lids as patterns, mark round on the lining material with chalk or pencil and cut out, allowing $\frac{1}{2}$ an inch all round for turnings. Four side-covers will be needed.

With untrimmed corners uppermost, lay each piece of card down on its lining, bring turnings over firmly and stick down so that no wrinkles or looseness spoil the smoothness of the right side. Prepare all sides and base of box and the thin card top in this manner. Neaten and trim corners where necessary.

With lined sides inside, oversew base and sides together to make box (Diagram 39).

Cut a strip from cover material 21 inches long by 3 inches wide. Check its length round box for fit and mark places for seams. Join the two ends and trim off surplus turnings, leaving about $\frac{1}{4}$ of an inch, and press.

Make a turning all round joined strip of $\frac{1}{4}$ of an inch and press down before pinning into position round upper

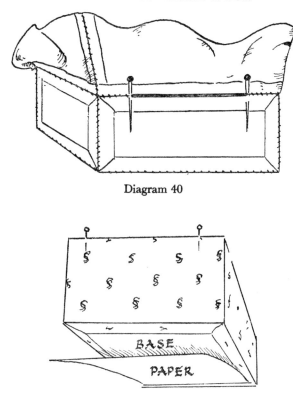

Diagram 40

Diagram 41

edge so that wrong side is on the outer side of box. Place
seam either centre back or on a corner.

Mark with a pin a distance $\frac{1}{2}$ an inch from each corner
at back of box. The space between will be left open for
hinge to slip in for sticking. Oversew covering all round to
top edge, then turn over and pull down firmly to hide the
sides to which lining has been stuck. Keep covering strip
taut and stick turnings down on to underside of box
(Diagram 40). Finally, hide these by sticking a square of
paper or thin card over the base (Diagram 41).

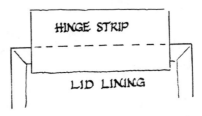

Diagram 42

To make a hinged lid

For the hinge, cut a strip of covering material $1\frac{1}{2}$ inches wide and twice the width of one side, allowing $\frac{1}{2}$ an inch for seam either end, join on the wrong side, trim off surplus and press. Turn right side out and press double.

Stick this firmly to one edge of the covered lining of the lid, overlapping by about $\frac{1}{2}$ an inch (Diagram 42).

When dry, stick lining with attached strip to wrong side of the already covered lid, so that the hinge lies smoothly between them (Diagram 43).

Finally, slip remaining side of double strip down between the two edges of the back, which has been left open. Make sure it is well down but that movement is easy without being loose, and stick to card side and also to outer cover. Slip-stitch or very fine oversewing to the latter makes for security and hard wear (Diagram 44).

Although this method seems complicated when set out step by step, it is a very satisfactory one and there is less room for error if all the pieces which make up the box are prepared separately, as opposed to cutting the base and sides from one piece of card and folding them into shape after scoring.

A piping-cord finish to the lid must be sewn or stuck to the edge before the lining card is placed in position. It is a particularly suitable finish for a box. Clip as much of the

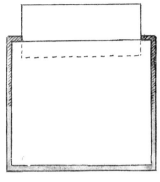

Diagram 43

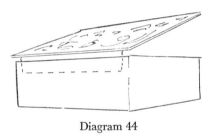

Diagram 44

surplus piping material away when going round corners, so that flatness is preserved.

Separate lids

These are sometimes preferred. A close-fitting one with a rim can be made on the same principle as the box just described. The strips of card for the sides of the lid must be cut to fit and should not be deeper than $\frac{1}{2}$ an inch. A strip of material long enough to go right round the square will be easier to fit on than four small strips sewn on separately.

D

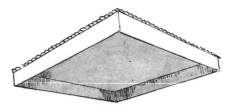

Diagram 45

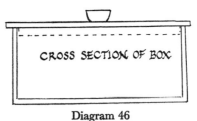

Diagram 46

A cord or couching to cover the joining seam on the edge of the lid is easy and practical (Diagram 45).

A separate lid of another type is one which fits the inside of the box top. This usually has a knob or ring fixed to make lifting off easy.

The inner fitting square, which will form the lining, can be made from fairly thick card or polystyrene. When cut out, this must be covered very neatly with lining material before being stuck into place inside the lid (Diagram 46).

A lid for the square box needs to have each side 5 2/10 inches in length. This should be enough to allow a narrow edge to protrude all round, plus the width of the card from which the box has been made, as well as the slight thicknesses of materials.

Cut the square of card so that the sides are 4 8/10 inches and try it for fit. Remember to allow for covering. It should fit well but not too tightly.

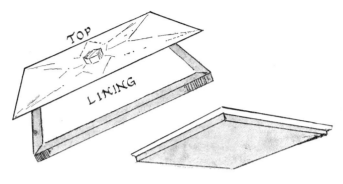

Diagram 47

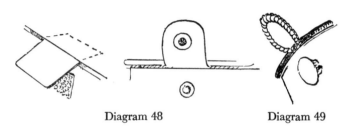

Diagram 48   Diagram 49

Cover the lid with material, bringing the turnings allowance well underneath and sticking down flatly. If a ring
or large bead is to be added for lifting, it should be fixed at
this stage. A knob can be made and stuck on afterwards.

Cover the small inside square with lining and stick wrong
side of lid, taking care to leave a narrow border of equal
width all round (Diagram 47).

A *knob* can be made by covering a small shaped piece
of polystyrene, or by stuffing a small circle of material
which has been gathered and drawn up tightly. Patches—
hexagon-shaped, joined two together and padded—also
make a good knob. These need stitching into place and
sticking to be really strong.

Fastenings, both press studs and velcro, necessitate a small tab being made to attach to the lid. This tab is inserted between lid and lining in the centre and stuck and stitched down (Diagram 48).

A loop and button fastening is fairly straightforward to fix, but it is only suitable for the daintiest type of box (Diagram 49).

Covering a ready-made circular box with fitted lid

This is rather quicker than making the box, but the same precision is needed during preparation.

Follow the diagram in taking the necessary measurements, but, before using the tape-measure to ascertain the distance round the box and lid, mark with a pencil where this is to start and finish. Divide the diameter by two to find the radius of both box and lid (Diagram 50).

With compasses set correctly, draw two circles on thin card, one the radius of the box, the other the radius of the lid. Cut out on the pencil line. Cover both neatly and smoothly with lining material. (If the lid is to be covered with patchwork or decorated with appliqué, a circle of stiff paper is a useful guide for the area to be covered.)

Measure and cut out a strip of thin card the length round the box and the same height. Fit it round inside so that the ends just meet, and trim off surplus. Cover it with lining material and oversew the two ends on wrong side to make a 'collar'.

Before doing this, with the strip of card as pattern, cut a similar piece of material for the outside cover, with the same allowances for turnings all round (Diagram 51).

Test for fit, join, trim and press; then, with right side towards you, stick top turnings down over rim of box and press smoothly round. Pull cover well down before sticking the turnings down on to base. In doing this, clip all surplus

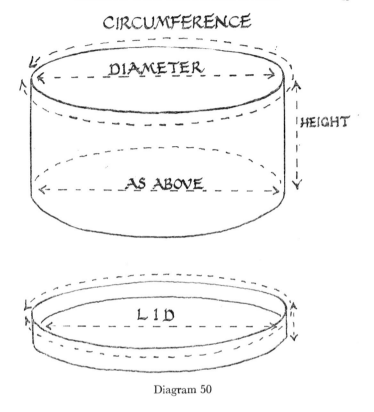

CIRCUMFERENCE

DIAMETER

AS ABOVE

HEIGHT

LID

Diagram 50

away so that the material lies quite flat. Neaten by sticking a circle of paper down to cover (Diagram 52).

To complete, slip 'collar' into place and stick and fit in the circle of prepared card.

Follow much the same procedure for the lid as for the box, covering the outer rim first, before slipping in and sticking the collar and card linings.

Finally, put top cover in position, covering yet another card circle, if this is one piece of material, and leaving papers in if a patchwork cover has been made.

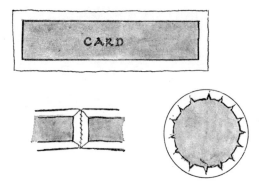

Diagram 51

Diagram 52   Diagram 53

Stitch round edge of rim to join covers (Diagram 53).

Where plastic materials are used for lining, it will not be necessary to sew joins. This can be done with adhesive or sellotape, on wrong side.

6. Making patchwork garments. Using patchwork decoratively

Surely there has never been a better time than the present one for exploring the possibilities of patchwork in this direction. Fashionable *and* sophisticated clothes lend themselves wholly or in part to patchwork.

Dress patterns for women and children have become very simple in style and it is decoration or accessories that add individuality and character. A colourful patchwork belt, with gleaming buckle, can do wonders for a dark dress or tunic, and a patchwork collar will accentuate a neck line. Patchwork motifs and borders can be applied to hemlines of both day and evening clothes and in the right materials will add glamour and a note of high fashion.

Ponchos, tunics and jerkins, all much in vogue, are easy styles and can be made entirely in patches or decorated with pieced or applied motifs.

For some of us, sleeves and facings can present a problem, and there is no reason why these should not be made in plain fabric, or knitted or crocheted, so long as the materials of which they are made tone in weight and colour. These are combinations which can look very good and be practical and time-saving.

Patchwork in the applied form can look very attractive against a plain or patterned background and can even provide a surface for further elaboration. This category of patchwork is a free-for-all and, so long as the chosen materials create the intended effect, anything may be used, including the full range of currently fashionable materials, from flimsiest gauze to leather.

In many of our markets, in both cities and small towns, one can frequently find a leather stall which sells ready-cut squares for patchwork. These look well made up as skirts and jerkins, as many teenagers have found. With the correct attachment, the pieces can be joined together by machine, yet handsewing, though more laborious, can produce a more elegant result. By passing the leather through an unthreaded machine, as if stitching, with the needle following the seam width, small evenly-spaced punctures are made, through which the stitches can be sewn easily. Strong cotton thread must be used for handsewing, with a short between needle 5 or 6.

Making a garment in patchwork

Choose a pattern in a simple style.

Cut out the lining and make up darts and shapings. However the lining is to be put in, this gives a surface on to which groups of patches may be pinned out for trial before joining together.

Paste the pattern on to strong paper to give a firm planning surface for designing.

Select your template(s), taking into consideration the type of garment to be made, the materials and the size and shape that seem best for the purpose and design. When thinking about the latter, be quite clear as to whether it is to be a repetitive, all-over pattern or one with a definite area framed within a plain, patched background.

If a definite pattern area is planned, it is a good idea to sketch this out roughly on the pattern pieces. These can be worked out as separate units before filling in with back-

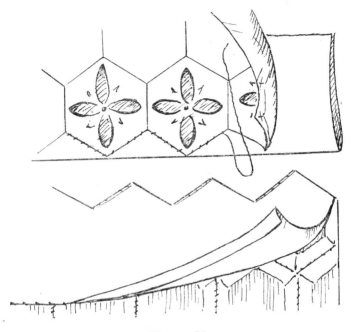

Diagram 54

ground patches. Hexagons, diamonds and church windows are a good choice as templates for garments. Darts and shapings can be made in the finished patchwork, just as for normal dressmaking, but it is often possible to adjust the patches to fit the shapings. This is particularly so when diamonds or church-window templates are chosen.

Seams may be handsewn, especially when the edges have been straightened with half-patches which are already turned over, but machine seams are quicker and more practical and will almost certainly stand up better to vigorous wear.

When the patchwork is finished, the usual processes must be gone through, as for any dressmaking. Avoid bulkiness

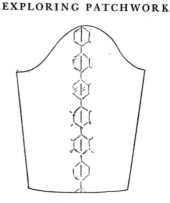

Diagram 55

on the hem by facing with a strip of plain material or even
a strip of patches to match outline of patchwork. This can
be decorative, too, as well as neat and strong. Lining edge
can be turned up to match the patches (Diagram 54).

Bear in mind that your garment is for wear. It must
keep its shape, for instance, and to ensure this it is sometimes sensible to line the patches with vilene. Thin card
will be necessary for 'papers' to make up tweeds and velvets.

When making sleeves in patchwork, it helps to centre a
line of patches (Diagram 55) before filling out the space
either side, building up the pattern until it fills the area.

It is no new thing to make clothing of patchwork.
Joseph's coat of many colours could have been made in it
and there are examples in variety from periods nearer our
own time, each possessing its own unique quality and
beauty.

7. Making a quilt

The planning and making of a quilt is a big undertaking and not every patchworker is attracted by the idea, particularly if she is a beginner. Eventually, however, a fair proportion of us are tempted and there can be no doubt that, in both England and America, there will be handed down as good a crop of patchwork quilts as we ourselves have inherited and treasured.

'Quilting' is still the very heart of American patchwork, though the designs are more likely to be applied than pieced. The traditional block patterns, made from patches and involving the use of templates, are still much sought after and new ones are still being made.

A knowledge of the history of the early days of Canada and America makes it easy to understand the reasons for the popularity of block quilts and why their patterns run into hundreds. When the early settlers undertook long journeys across country, the small compact patchwork blocks were far more convenient to work at or transport than a bed-cover which grew increasingly large and bulky. Patterns could easily be copied and exchanged, as indeed they were, and the original name frequently altered in the process. It must have meant a great deal in those uneasy, difficult times for those first American women to meet and exchange quilting ideas. It is moving to reflect that courage and endurance, as well as friendship, must have contributed to the creation of the designs and the quilts made from them.

The television Western reminds us how important this craft was in the furnishing of the settler's home, for almost every one gives us a glimpse of a quilt—and no two patterns ever seem to be alike. The family and communal traditions connected with quilting speeded up the provision of those needed to supply a home, in addition to giving opportunities for learning fresh skills and gathering ideas. Today, this pleasant tradition continues and quilting picnics and exhibitions are a popular part of American country life.

In England, too, many old quilts were a combined family effort. There is a beautiful patchwork coverlet made by Jane Austen and her mother and sisters. Those who took the craft to America no doubt must have found it an obvious means of supplying as quickly as possible the warm bedcovers that were so urgently needed to withstand the severe winters.

Plate 19 shows a modern English example of communal work. The design was created by one person, who also made the pictorial centre, 'Morning, noon and night', while the border, involving the signs of the zodiac, was the work of several Northamptonshire W.I. members. The coverlet is made entirely in patchwork.

As American life became settled, and homes more elegant, quilts made in appliqué became popular. For these, too, block patterns were designed and were in frequent use, alternating with quilted blocks of plain colour to accentuate their pattern. There were also many made in a variety of designs which filled the complete area of the quilt. Some of the most beautiful work of this kind, both in America and England, has come from this mid-eighteenth- to early nineteenth-century period.

Border quilts were fashionable in England in the first half of the nineteenth century. These were designed and made with alternating borders of patchwork and appliqué.

In parts of England and Wales where quilting was traditional, the two crafts were frequently combined.

Appliqué as such is seldom seen on English coverlets today, though the beautiful bird designs on those made by Miss D. M. Crampton of Somerset are unique examples of traditional appliqué. This twin sister of patchwork has strayed into other fields and is more likely to be found in fabric pictures or creative embroidery. In its traditional form, it is still used in ecclesiastical work. Machine embroidery has superseded the hand-stitching of herringbone and blanket-stitch that was once used to cover the unturned edges of the applied shapes. It is quicker and can look as delightful. In this modern treatment, the basic principles of the craft still obtain.

The quilt

The term 'quilt' is frequently applied to what is more truly a coverlet or bedcover. A quilt should have a warm interlining and when this is in place quilting has been proved to be the best method of keeping it there.

Forethought and careful planning is essential in preparations for making a quilt or coverlet, which will, after all, be the centre of interest in the room whose bed it covers. The colour scheme will be influenced by the setting, if this is known in advance. Both materials and colours will be chosen accordingly and perhaps the design will bear some relationship to some of the furnishings. A sophisticated design, for instance, might be out of place in a simple country bedroom. Colour choice may be influenced by the aspect of a room: lively, warm colours will brighten a north room, while cooler shades can look charming in a sunny room.

The size of bed must also be taken into account, so that in both design and colour there is the right balance. Try to remember this at all the planning stages. It would be wrong to concentrate colour in the centre of the coverlet and use only weak tones at the border. When the 'line' of the design has been worked out, it helps to cut out the shapes of pattern areas in newspaper and try them on a bed of the right size, using it as a working surface. Coloured paper used in conjunction with the newspaper helps with colour balance.

The focal points of the design should be placed where they are most likely to be appreciated. For example, the design for a child's bedcover is a merry-go-round surrounded by figures : the place for the merry-go-round is either the centre of the bed or the pillow, while the dancing figures can form a border round the mattress edge or be grouped in such a way that they indicate the focal point.

A sketch, no matter how rough, is really helpful at this stage : squared or isometric paper is very useful if the coverlet is to be patchwork. Coloured pens or paint help with definitions of pattern.

Materials

These should, of course, be new. It is foolhardy to use worn materials for something which it is hoped will be beautiful and long-lasting. This is the time when it must be bought by the yard, particularly for the plain colours and the lining. Amounts will be decided by the design and type of quilt or coverlet.

To quote from Ruby McKim's 101 *Patchwork Patterns*: 'Mainstay of patchwork, 1700–75—calico; from 1775–1825—calico; from 1825–75—calico', and to that we could add, 'from 1875–1972—calico', or at least our modern versions of it. Time and usage have proved the worth of good, firmly-woven cotton materials for any type of patchwork. There are a variety to choose from in patterned fabrics, especially sateens and chintzes, percales, prints and poplins, but it is becoming more and more difficult to buy plain colours in pure cotton fibres.

Texture should play an important part when large areas of plain colour are planned. It adds interest where monotony could prevail. Very small spotted and checked fabrics can be equally useful for this purpose, so long as their tonal values blend in with the rest. Using these cleverly can be as much fun as planning the main design.

Sewing thread

For sewing thread, cotton is best. It should not be coarser than 50 or 60; 80 and 100 are both suitable. 'Drima', a superspun polyester thread, frequently has to take the place of fine cotton, which is not always easy to find. Though good for sewing, its life span is as yet unknown.

Needles must also be fine—7, 8 or 9.

Templates

There is a tendency in these modern times to choose large templates for coverlets, because the work grows more quickly. This may be true, but there is a limit beyond which it is not wise to go, unless one is sure of one's skill as a designer. It may help to list some suggested sizes for patchwork:

Hexagons, church windows, octagons: $\frac{3}{4}$ inch to $1\frac{1}{2}$ inches
Diamonds: $1\frac{1}{4}$ inches to 2 inches

All these are a suitable choice for a double or single bed, so long as they 'fit in' with the patterned material. For cot covers, $\frac{1}{2}$–$\frac{3}{4}$ of an inch templates are daintier. In any case, one must relate one's templates to the pattern of material and the design to be made from it, as well as the size of the coverlet.

A Victorian lady made thirteen coverlets for friends and family, all of them in half-inch hexagons. It is a matter of taste!

Even after the most meticulous planning, ideas can change as work progresses, and it is advisable from time to time to try out the effect of one's patchwork or appliqué on a bed of the correct size, laying out the pieces in the positions they will occupy as part of the bedcover. Most of us tend to join up pattern areas before the background is filled in. This method is as useful for block-patterned 'rosette' and 'lozenge' quilts as it is for one involving larger units of design. When background material can be thrown across the bed first, then the colour values can be better seen.

One of the great advantages of making a quilt in appliqué is that from start to finish the work is pliable and easy to handle. Not so the one made in patchwork and therefore stiffened by the paper linings. These linings need not all remain in place to the end, but enough can be removed to make the joining-up proceed comfortably, though patches round the edge should keep their papers until work is finished.

Completing the quilt

Most appeals for advice come under this heading, but plans for the finishing should be made at the initial stages, before work is even begun.

The lining material will be chosen to fit in with the general scheme in colour and weight. It should be cut on the straight (i.e., with the grain) and, since most suitable fabrics are 36 inches wide, any joins must be made before fitting. When an interlining is included, it must be tacked (basted) on to the wrong side of the patchwork before it is covered by the lining.

11 and 12. Two sides of workbag in yellow, black and white and grey cottons. *Author.*

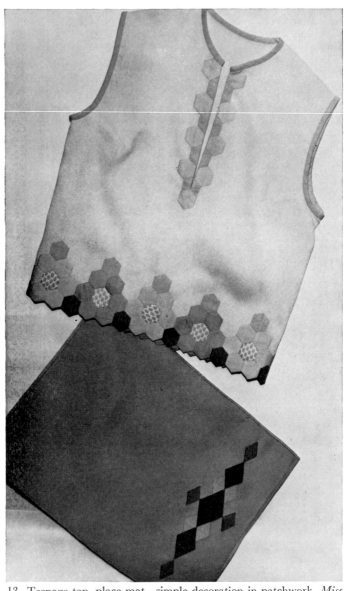

13. Teenage top, place mat—simple decoration in patchwork. *Miss Anne Dyer.*

14. Borders in patchwork and appliqué on two aprons. *Miss E. Bicknell, Westmorland, and Author.*

15. Evening cloak in satin and brocades, multi-coloured. *Mrs P. Lyon, Caernarvonshire.*

16. Cotton mini-dress—navy, turquoise and pink. *Miss G. Collings, Leics. and Rutland.*

17. Tunic—bright pinks, greens and deep blue. *Mrs Ashmore.*

18. Modern log cabin—black, blue, green and white. *Miss Anne Dyer.*

19. Quilt for Northamptonshire Denman College bedroom. Border, greys and off white; appropriate colours for seasons and day and night sections. *Mrs Ashmore and other Northamptonshire W.I. members.*

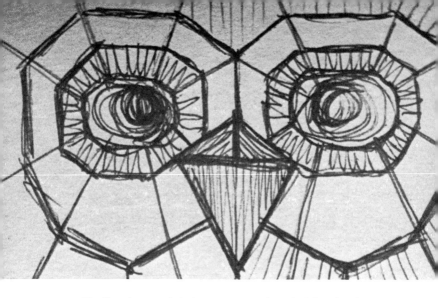

20. Sketch for owl design in free patchwork. *Miss Anne Dyer.*

21. Centre of cushion made from owl design. *Miss Anne Dyer.*

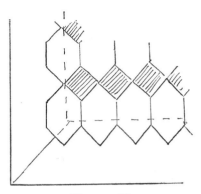

Diagram 56

Modern beds are of a standard size and a coverlet or quilt for a 3-feet single bed needs to be 72 inches wide. A 4 feet 6 inches double bed needs a coverlet or quilt 90 inches wide. Both sizes should be 108 inches long. These measurements are suitable for a full-size coverlet.

Before the edges are finished, preparations must be made. Pressing must be done, from the right side in the case of patchwork, and after tackings and papers have been taken out. Edges may need to be straightened.

To give a crisp firm edge, there is nothing better than a piping cord, and this must be finely slip-stitched on to the patchwork before the lining goes on by the same method. A cord about $\frac{1}{4}$ inch in diameter is a good average thickness and may be of pre-shrunk cotton or nylon. Material for piping should be $1\frac{1}{2}$ inches to $2\frac{1}{2}$ inches wide—enough to cover the cord and allow a little less than $\frac{1}{2}$ inch for insertion when fitted. Any surplus can be trimmed off afterwards before the lining is sewn. Although handsewing takes longer than machine-sewing, it gives the best results, for the fine close slip-stitches, lying close to the piping cord, are hidden.

When the patchwork is mounted on to the lining in such

B

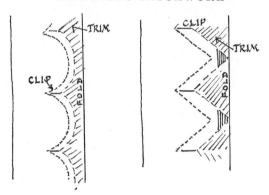

Diagram 57

a way that the unstraightened but turned-over patches are stitched down on to a wide hem, a very attractive, neat finish is achieved. The lining should be cut with a wide enough allowance to turn on to the right side and be covered by the patchwork edges, leaving a border of plain material all round. Corners should be mitred (Diagram 56).

A scalloped or vandyke edging can be made by marking out a double strip into even spaces and drawing in with chalk or pencil the shapes to be machine-sewn on the material. A ruler is needed for the straight lines of the vandykes; any firm, circular article will do duty for a template for the scallops (Diagram 57).

Mark out on the wrong side and machine-sew before turning to right side and pressing. Take care to make points or scallops proportionate to the size of the quilt. $1\frac{1}{2}$ yards of material cut on the bias should be sufficient to supply scalloped or vandyke borders for an average quilt.

Binding is more frequently seen on an appliquéd quilt than a patchwork one. It gives a neat, practical finish and emphasises the limits of the coverlet. It can be effectively used to mark out certain areas or unite the blocks. The width is a matter of taste and balance. The lining must be

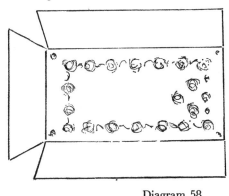
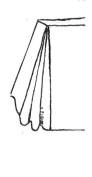

Diagram 58

tacked into place before either a flat or rolled binding is
put round.

A fitted coverlet is often preferred to a 'spread', because
the area to be made in patchwork only covers the top of
the mattress and is therefore quicker to finish. It looks
well on the modern divan bed, whether made in patchwork
or appliqué. A deep, plain valance is needed, in addition to
the lining, and whether pleated or plain it is easy to
launder, as the diagram indicates (Diagram 58).

A border of pattern sewn on to the bottom hem of a
plain valance is an attractive way of linking up with the
main design.

Fringes are to be used with discretion. They should
never be fussy or elaborate. Plain white cotton ones look
best, for they are firm enough to make a definite edge and
they launder well.

It is sound sense to avoid any type of fussy finish, and
frills come into this category, unless they are the narrow-
pleated variety, which can look very good in the right
place.

Except where binding is used, lining the quilt is the final
process. The lining is there to neaten the back, to strengthen

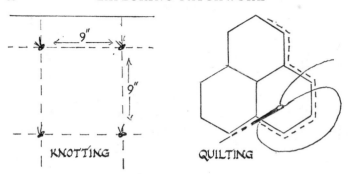

KNOTTING   QUILTING

Diagram 59

the work and to keep it in shape. It should fit exactly and once again the floor may come into use as the best place for fitting and pinning. Tacking (basting) should be thorough before the final sewing. Bindings and fringes can quite well be machine-sewn, but handsewing has its place and lasts long.

The last detail of all is quilting or knotting the lining to the right side. A frame is the ideal means of quilting, but as only a comparatively small amount may be needed, equally good results can be achieved by laying both surfaces very carefully and precisely together, and then tacking with equal care. Alternatively, there is knotting, which is practical and quick. Imagine the quilt divided all over into 9-inch or 12-inch squares and, from the lining side, with a needleful of double thread, stitch through at each intersection and back again, tying the four ends tightly in a reef knot. Cut off, leaving a tuft at least $\frac{1}{8}$ of an inch long. This gives the knot a long life (Diagram 59).

When the quilt is completed, use it. There must be thousands of unfinished ones in the world, so to have completed one is a real achievement. A great deal of thought and effort has contributed to its making; if it is well made, then be proud of it and enjoy your handiwork.

8. Modern trends and ideas

The history of patchwork is an excellent demonstration of how the development of a craft is influenced by great events and social conditions. Materials which were available at particular periods, as well as the skills of different generations of craftswomen, have made their contribution.

Patchwork as a craft began to make a strong comeback immediately after the Second World War and was already popular by the time Yves St Laurent made use of it in *haute couture,* stimulating interest among many people who had previously barely heard of it. Today, its popularity is widespread and those who do patchwork find it both enjoyably relaxing and profitable. So many are discovering that thriftiness can lead to beauty and how deeply satisfying this can be.

In the second half of the 20th century, patchwork is at the peak of its revival. It is being taught in many schools as part of needlework or creative sessions. Colleges of art include it in fashion design and embroidery. It is a popular subject in Further Education classes and many who learn it continue to do patchwork in their homes, enjoying the relaxation it brings and the convenience of a craft which can fit so well into the demands of everyday life, being so easily taken up and worked on, and put down as occasion demands.

The therapeutic qualities of so absorbing a craft are recognised by those who work among the mentally ill. In homes for the elderly, a patchwork coverlet can provide entertainment for a bedridden person. There are many of us who have found patchwork a panacea to help us through difficult, anxious times. Long nights have been shortened because there were patches to make and a pattern to work out.

This must have been so since patchwork began, for in every sense it is a homecraft which, for those who love it, reflects their life and becomes interwoven with it.

Like others before us, we in our time are abiding by the tried basic principles, and by interpreting them in our modern idiom are adding new and exciting trends to be passed on to succeeding generations.

It is now acknowledged that, in good patchwork, colour and design are every bit as important as technical excellence. The principle of cutting all patches with the grain of the material, once so rigidly observed, has at last been relaxed, as it had to be once the importance of design was recognised. What frustrations it must have caused when slavishly followed! There is little fear that patches will lose shape when the right type of material has been used and joining seams are well sewn. In spite of the truth of this, it should be remembered that certain shapes are more easily constructed when cut on the grain, bearing in mind also the decorative use that can be made of textures in plain materials.

Although a great deal of modern patchwork is traditional in character, an impressive amount is being produced that is adventurously original. Just as the Victorians used their sprigged and beflowered patterns and rich or gentle colours to make their patchwork quilts, so in our age the brilliant and sometimes revolutionary colour combinations in contemporary design are putting their stamp on our work. The proportion of quilts may be fewer, but accessories for the home and our personal use are being made in quantity.

Noteworthy among these are the decorative hangings

and pictures using free design. The head of an owl (Plate 21) forms the centre of a cushion and, in spite of its original treatment, is true patchwork. The outline sketch (Plate 20) shows how the shapes were arrived at which, when joined, made up the bird's mask. The picture of the completed patchwork is full of 'owlish' character. Pictures in patchwork are not new but those from other periods have usually been made in appliqué. In either form of patchwork, they are fun to do and offer scope for originality.

All sincerely creative craftsmen know 'the joy of bringing beauty into the world, of seeing it emerge, of feeling part of it'. Even the beginner in patchwork can appreciate the truth of these words.

Ideas are always being sought for designs and colour schemes. Often there are surprising relationships between one craft and another, so it is worthwhile looking for inspiration in books which apparently could have nothing to offer for patchwork. Those on rugs, carpets or tiles, as well as others on more obviously related crafts, such as embroidery, fabric printing or weaving, show patterns which can be frequently developed. Tiles are made in template shapes and decorated ones in churches and museums are good sources of ideas. It is useful to carry a small notebook to copy these. Colour schemes will be suggested, too, and china and pottery can help here, as can fabrics, which might also provide examples of balanced colour schemes.

Window-dressing is an art and lighting is a contributory factor in gaining an effect. An exciting window display can inspire not only ideas for colour but also textures. Wallpaper designers frequently reflect patchwork popularity in their patterns, and these can effectively be reproduced in the craft they imitate.

One can suggest sources endlessly, but the fact is that, once bitten by the patchwork 'bug', we find that ideas are all about us, and before long we develop the 'seeing eye' which is at the heart of all true craftmanship.

Suppliers of equipment

Templates can be obtained from :
  J. E. M. Patchwork Templates,
  18 St. Helen's Street,
  Cockermouth,
  Cumberland.
  Their catalogue, illustrated in colour, 20p at the time of writing, gives details of sets 11 and 12 and other useful information.
  For slender-stemmed clamshells, as well as other shapes :
  Rowe and Son,
  The Market Place,
  Ripon, Yorks.
  or
  The Needlewoman Shop,
  146 Regent Street,
  London, W1.
Fine sewing cotton (60, 80 and 100) has to be sought out and is in very short supply. *Drima* is a good substitute and can be bought from many local stores.

Recommended books

Patchwork Quilts, Averil Colby. Batsford, London
Old Patchwork Quilts, Ruth Finley (reissued). Charles T. Branford Co., Newton, Mass., and G. Bell and Sons, London
Quilt Making and Collecting, Marguerite Ickis. Greystone Press, New York

Mounting Handicraft, Grete Kronke. Van Nostrand Reinholt Co., New York and London

Designs for Craftsmen, Walter Miles. Doubleday, New York

101 *Patchwork Patterns,* Ruby Short McKim. Leman Publications, Wheatridge, Colorado

Patchwork Today: *A Practical Introduction,* Doris E. Marston. G. Bell and Sons, London, and Charles T. Branford Co., Newton, Mass.

Index